HÄGAR THE HORRIBLE: SMOTHERLY LOVE

There may be some argument about which European first discovered America — an Italian or a Viking. But now the whole world has discovered that jolly Viking, Hägar the Horrible.

Hägar is back with his entire Viking crew plus Helga, Honi, Hamlet, Snert, Kvack and, of course, Lucky Eddie, Hägar's sidekick.

Here's your chance to join the more than 100 million people who "discovered" and enjoy Hägar every day, in over 1600 newspapers around the world.

Hägar's creator is Dik Browne, twice winner of the Reuben Award, the National Cartoonist Society's highest honor.

Hägar the Horrible Books

HÄGAR THE HORRIBLE
HÄGAR THE HORRIBLE: ANIMAL HAUS
HÄGAR THE HORRIBLE: BORN LEADER
HÄGAR THE HORRIBLE: BRING 'EM BACK ALIVE
HÄGAR THE HORRIBLE: THE BRUTISH ARE COMING
HÄGAR THE HORRIBLE: EXCUSE ME!
HÄGAR THE HORRIBLE: HAVE YOU BEEN UPTIGHT LATELY?
HÄGAR THE HORRIBLE: HÄGAR HITS THE MARK
HÄGAR THE HORRIBLE: HÄGAR'S KNIGHT OUT
HÄGAR THE HORRIBLE: HANDYMAN SPECIAL
HÄGAR THE HORRIBLE: HAPPY HOUR
HÄGAR THE HORRIBLE: HELGA'S REVENGE
HÄGAR: HI, DEAR, YOUR HAIR LOOKS GREAT!
HÄGAR THE HORRIBLE: HORNS OF PLENTY
HÄGAR THE HORRIBLE: MIDNIGHT MUNCHIES
HÄGAR THE HORRIBLE: MY FEET ARE DRUNK
HÄGAR THE HORRIBLE: THE NORD STAR
HÄGAR THE HORRIBLE: NORSE CODE
HÄGAR THE HORRIBLE: ON THE LOOSE
HÄGAR THE HORRIBLE: ON THE RACK
HÄGAR THE HORRIBLE: ROMAN HOLIDAY
HÄGAR THE HORRIBLE: SACK TIME
HÄGAR THE HORRIBLE: THE SIMPLE LIFE
HÄGAR THE HORRIBLE: SMOTHERLY LOVE
HÄGAR THE HORRIBLE: SPRING CLEANING
HÄGAR THE HORRIBLE: STRAPPED FOR CASH

HÄGAR® THE HORRIBLE

by DIK BROWNE

SMOTHERLY LOVE

JOVE BOOKS, NEW YORK

HÄGAR THE HORRIBLE: SMOTHERLY LOVE

A Jove Book / published by arrangement with
King Features Syndicate, Inc.

PRINTING HISTORY
Jove edition / July 1989

For information address: The Berkley Publishing Group,
200 Madison Avenue, New York, New York 10016.

ISBN: 0-515-10144-3

Jove Books are published by The Berkley Publishing Group,
200 Madison Avenue, New York, New York 10016.
The name "JOVE" and the "J" logo
are trademarks belonging to Jove Publications, Inc.

PRINTED IN THE UNITED STATES OF AMERICA

10 9 8 7 6 5 4 3 2 1

MEN CAN'T HANDLE THE IDEA OF A WOMAN WITH POWER
10·21 DIK BROWNE
© 1987 King Features Syndicate, Inc. World rights reserved

MEN, A SPY HAS MANAGED TO INFILTRATE OUR RANKS!

...A VERY DUMB SPY, AS IT TURNS OUT

STUPID! THE SHIP SINKS, AND WHAT'S THE ONE THING HE SAVES ??
10-23

AN ICE BUCKET!

DR. ZOOK IS FAMOUS FOR HIS "NOSE JOBS"
I KNOW...
© 1987 King Features Syndicate, Inc. World rights reserved

DIK BROWNE 10-24
HE DID MINE

OH, WELL... TOMORROW'S ANOTHER DAY

REALLY ?! WHAT'S IT CALLED ?
10-26
DIK BROWNE

HOW DID YOUR EARS GET SO DIRTY ?!

HAVE YOU BEEN LISTENING TO THOSE STUPID STORIES THAT MEN TELL ?
DIK BROWNE
10-27

I KNOW THIS CHARACTER INSIDE AND OUT

OUT IS BETTER!
10·28
DIK BROWNE

MIRROR, MIRROR, ON THE WALL – WHO'S THE FAIREST OF THEM ALL ?
© 1987 King Features Syndicate, Inc. World rights reserved

I DON'T KNOW... I CAN'T SEE... MOVE OVER !
DIK BROWNE
10·29

I NEVER KNEW REAL-ESTATE AGENTS WERE SO COMPETITIVE
FOR SALE
© 1987 King Features Syndicate, Inc. World rights reserved
DIK BROWNE 10-30

IT'S AWFUL TO BE PUSHING 30

IT'S WORSE TO BE *PULLING* IT !!
10-31

HOW CAN THE STORK FIND HIS WAY BACK TO US EVERY YEAR WITHOUT FAIL ?
GOD KNOWS

I THINK YOU'RE RIGHT
11-2
DIK BROWNE

HAPPY HOUR IS OVER IN 5 MINUTES!
© 1987 King Features Syndicate Inc. World rights reserved

NOBODY EVER HANDED ME ANYTHING! ANYTHING I EVER GOT I GOT MYSELF!
DIK BROWNE

THANKS, DEAR... AND CAN YOU GET ME A BEER ?
11-4

© 1987 King Features Syndicate Inc World rights reserved
THIS IS OLE OLSON... THE CHECKER CHAMPION!
11-5 DIK BROWNE

BROWNE
HMMMMM...

WAKE UP!!

YOU WERE DAYDREAMING AGAIN
11-6

WHY DO THEY CALL YOU LUCKY EDDIE ?
IT WAS MY FATHER'S NAME. WHY DO THEY CALL YOU RICHARD THE THIRD ?

SAME REASON...
YOUR FATHER'S NAME WAS "LUCKY EDDIE"?
DIK BROWNE 11-7

PSST!!
11-9 DIK BROWNE
© 1987 King Features Syndicate, Inc. World rights reserved

BOY, I REALLY HAD A HECTIC DAY! MY NERVES ARE SHOT!!
© 1987 King Features Syndicate, Inc. World rights reserved
DO I HAVE TIME TO RELAX AND HAVE A LEISURELY DRINK BEFORE DINNER?
DIK BROWNE 11-10
YES, IF YOU HURRY

DID YOU PUT THE WHOOPEE CUSHION UNDER THE SEAT?
TEE HEE
DIK BROWNE 11-11
© 1987 King Features Syndicate, Inc. World rights reserved

KOYER! SOME LAWYER YOU TURNED OUT TO BE!
HEY! I FOUND A LOOPHOLE, DIDN'T I ?

THIS ISN'T THE SORT OF **LOOPHOLE** I WAS LOOKING FOR!
11-12 DIK BROWNE

THAT'S UNFAIR! YOU CAN'T LUMP ALL MEN TOGETHER!
YOU'RE RIGHT!

SOME ARE LUMPIER
DIK BROWNE 11-13

ARTICHOKE... AVOCADOS...
ASPARAGUS...
© 1987 King Features Syndicate, Inc. World rights reserved

DIK BROWNE
WHY ARE ALL THE "A" VEGETABLES SO WEIRD ?
11-14

CAN YOU FIND MY SOCKS?
I'LL TRY

DIK BROWNE 11-16
SARCASM!

A TEST OF WILLS
© 1987 King Features Syndicate, Inc. World rights reserved

VICTORY
DIK BROWNE 11-17

HOW DO YOU GET DADDY TO EAT HIS VEGETABLES ?
SIMPLY...

I USE THE CARROT AND STICK APPROACH
DIK BROWNE 11-18

WHY DO VIKINGS WEAR HATS ALL THE TIME ?
PRIDE!
TRADITION!
HAIR LOSS
DIK BROWNE
11-19
© 1987 King Features Syndicate, Inc. World rights reserved

YES, I CAN READ IT — BUT IT'S BORING AND I CAN'T FOLLOW THE STORY !
E
AO
DPFC
ITOHFP
NLZECLN
DIK BROWNE 11-20
© 1987 King Features Syndicate, Inc. World rights reserved

BLAM!
HELGA?!

GOOD! NOW THAT I HAVE YOUR ATTENTION...
11-21

OH, GOOD! THE SKI LIFT IS WORKING
DIK BROWNE 11-23
©1987 King Features Syndicate Inc. World rights reserved

THIS HOUSE COULD USE A GOOD CLEANING FOR THE HOLIDAYS

IT WAS JUST A COMMENT
DIK BROWNE
11-24

SNERT, GO IN AND SEE IF HELGA IS STILL ANGRY. IF SHE IS, BARK 3 TIMES!
VOOF!

HE'S NOT BARKING—IT MUST BE SAFE TO GO IN!
DIK BROWNE 11-25

OH, GOOD, DADDY'S GOING TO CARVE
DIK BROWNE
11-26
© 1987 King Features Syndicate, Inc. World rights reserved

WHAT MAKES A SUCCESSFUL MARRIAGE?
WELL...
© 1987 King Features Syndicate, Inc. World rights reserved

THE MOST IMPORTANT THING IS MUTUAL RESPECT
DIK BROWNE
11-27

NIGHTY NIGHT...
© 1987 King Features Syndicate, Inc. World rights reserved
SHHHH...
MY FOOT'S ASLEEP
DIK BROWNE
11-25

© 1987 King Features Syndicate, Inc. World rights reserved
ALL I CAUGHT WAS A ROTTEN LITTLE HEAD COLD!

BUT I ALMOST CAUGHT A BIG CASE OF PNEUMONIA!
FISHERMEN!!
11-30
DIK BROWNE

ANOTHER TOLL ?!
WHAT'S THIS ONE FOR ?!
TOLL
DIK BROWNE

TO FINISH THE BRIDGE
12-1

HAGAR! YOU'RE HERE TOO?! THIS IS GREAT!

WE CAN BE ROOMIES!!!
12-2

HAGAR, THOSE GUYS OVER THERE ARE MAKING FUN OF MY SENSE OF DIRECTION AS THE SHIP'S NAVIGATOR!
YOU MEAN THOSE GUYS OVER THERE?
ER... YES, THOSE GUYS OVER THERE
DIK BROWNE 12-3

WALKING THE DOG IS A DRAG!
BUT IT'S GOOD EXERCISE

BUT IT'S STILL A DRAG!!
KEEP OFF
DIK BROWNE 12-4

I WISH YOU'D DO SOMETHING ABOUT THAT OLD HAT... IT DOESN'T LOOK TOO SHARP

12-5
DIK BROWNE

WOW! A RINGER!
SHHHH!

YOU'LL WAKE DADDY UP
DIK BROWNE 12-7

I DON'T WANT YOU TO THINK OF ME AS YOUR BOSS, THINK OF ME AS YOUR FRIEND
© 1987 King Features Syndicate, Inc. World rights reserved
THINK OF ME AS YOUR BOSS

MAYBE WE SHOULD WAIT UNTIL AFTER THE WEDDING
DIK BROWNE 12-9
© 1987 King Features Syndicate, Inc. World rights reserved

MOM, DAD SAID MONOGAMY IS A TYPE OF WOOD
NO...
© 1987 King Features Syndicate, Inc. World rights reserved
DIK BROWNE
MONOGAMY IS WHEN YOU MARRY ONE PERSON FOR LIFE
YOUR FATHER'S ***HEAD*** IS A KIND OF WOOD...
12-10

HOW OLD ARE YOU, HELGA ?
LATE THIRTIES
CAN YOU BE MORE SPECIFIC ?
VERY LATE THIRTIES
DIK BROWNE 12-11
FORTY-TWO

ALL I WANT IS YOUR RESPECT, YOUR LOVE, YOUR ADMIRATION...
WHY SHOULD I GIVE YOU ANY OF THAT?

PITY?
DIK BROWNE
12-12

DADDY IS COMING!

DIK BROWNE
12-14
CHRISTMAS IS COMING

PIZZA—BEER—CAKE! HAGAR! HOW COULD YOU?!!

I HAD HELP
DIK BROWNE
12-15

HOCKEY IS SO VIOLENT
YOU THINK THIS IS VIOLENT ?

WAIT TILL THE GAME STARTS !
12-16
DIK
BROWNE

HELGA, REMEMBER, WE PROMISED WE'D NEVER GO TO BED ANGRY!
KNOCK KNOCK
YOU'RE RIGHT. YOU GET THE COUCH!
12-17

WHAT ARE YOU ?
I'M A WRITER
WHAT DO YOU WRITE ?
Fairy Tales, Fantasy and Fiction
DO YOU EVER DO INCOME TAX RETURNS ?
2-18
DIK BROWNE

THIS IS THE LAST YEAR WE'RE GOING TO YOUR MOTHER'S FOR CHRISTMAS!

THE HOLIDAY TRAFFIC GETS WORSE EVERY YEAR!
DIK BROWNE 12-19

YOU HAVE A LOT OF "PANACHE," MR. HAGAR
ER... THANKS

DIK BROWNE 12-21
SORRY ABOUT THAT...

HAGAR! COME HERE QUICK!
DIK BROWNE
YOU SAID NO TWO SNOWFLAKES WERE ALIKE — LOOK!
12-22
AW, SHUCKS!

DAD, IS IT FUN TO BE A GROWN-UP ?

HOW WOULD **I** KNOW?!
12·23
DIK BROWNE

SHOULD WE OPEN OUR GIFTS TOMORROW OR...
DIK BROWNE

...TONIGHT ?
12-24

CAN A TWINKLE MAKE A SOUND?
WHY DO YOU ASK?

I THINK I HEARD A STAR
DIK BROWNE 12·25

I'M THROUGH PUTTING IT OFF, FOOLIN' AROUND

THE DIET STARTS NEXT MONTH
12-26
DIK BROWNE

YOUR TROUBLE IS YOU TAKE EVERYTHING PERSONALLY
IS THAT THE TRUTH?
IT'S AS PLAIN AS THE NOSE ON YOUR FACE
THERE YOU GO AGAIN!!
DIK BROWNE
12-28

WHAT A DAY I HAD! DO I HAVE TIME FOR A DRINK BEFORE DINNER?
YES

GOOD! I'LL BE DOWN AT THE TAVERN
DIK BROWNE 12-29

DOES THIS DRESS LOOK TOO DULL FOR THE DANCE ?
MAYBE WE COULD JAZZ IT UP WITH SOME ACCESSORIES
DIK BROWNE
© 1987 King Features Syndicate, Inc. World rights reserved

THERE! DOESN'T THAT LOOK BETTER ?
12-30

YOU'VE BOTH MET ALBERT— MY "INSIGNIFICANT OTHER"
12-31
© 1987 King Features Syndicate, Inc. World rights reserved

HAPPY NEW YEA
OH DEAR, NOBODY TOUCHED MY CHEESE DIP!
DIK BROWNE
© 1987 King Features Syndicate, Inc. World rights reserved

YOU KNOW WHAT I NEED ? I NEED LESS CLUTTER IN MY LIFE.
UH HUH

WHY ARE YOU LOOKING AT ME ?!
1-2
DIK BROWNE

DADDY, WHAT'S AN OPTIMIST ?
DIK BROWNE 1-4
© 1988 King Features Syndicate, Inc. World rights reserved

YOU'VE GOT TO CHANGE YOUR WAYS!
SNAF
GRRR
UKK...

DIK BROWNE
SHUT UP! I'M TALKING TO HIM — NOT TO YOU!
GRRR...
UM..
1-5

I HATE IT WHEN THEY OVERBOOK ON THE HOLIDAYS!
DIK BROWNE
1-6
© 1988 King Features Syndicate Inc. World rights reserved

WHERE DID I COME FROM ?
THE STORK BROUGHT YOU
AND HONI ?
THE STORK BROUGHT HER
AND DAD ?
FOUR BIG STORKS
DIK BROWNE 1-7

WHERE'S MY...
IN THE TOP MIDDLE KITCHEN DRAWER NEXT TO THE GRATER AND UNDER THE BLUE TOWEL

I HATE WOMEN. THEY ALWAYS SEEM TO KNOW WHERE EVERYTHING IS!
DIK BROWNE 1-8

PLINK!

BAM!
BZK!
DIK BROWNE
1-9

TOUCHÉ

HELGA TALKS TO HOUSE PLANTS
DOES IT WORK ?
DIK BROWNE 1-11
© 1988 King Features Syndicate Inc World rights reserved

IT DOES FOR HELGA !
STAND UP! AND STOP DROPPING YOUR LEAVES!

HEY, DON'T I KNOW YOU?
1-12
© 1988 King Features Syndicate, Inc. World rights reserved

SVEN, I'D LIKE YOU TO MEET THE TOUGHEST, BRAVEST, SMARTEST PERSON I KNOW

AND THIS IS HER HUSBAND, HAGAR THE HORRIBLE
DIK BROWNE
1-13

HOW'S BUSINESS ?
DOWN, VERY DOWN
GOOD!
DIK BROWNE
HE MAKES A GREAT PILLOW
1-14

ALL HAMLET'S FRIENDS SAY HE'S THE NICEST BOY IN THE VILLAGE

WELL, HAGAR—
YOU KNOW HOW CRUEL KIDS CAN BE
DIK BROWNE 1-15

THIS IS KILLING ME!
IS THAT ARMOR VERY UNCOMFORTABLE?
DIK BROWNE

NAW! MY WIFE STARCHED MY SHORTS!
1-16

WOULD YOU LIKE A LIGHT SNACK ?
SURE! HOW ABOUT A BIG OL' HAM WITH A HONEY GLAZE AND RAISINS ?

DIK BROWNE
HOW ABOUT JUST THE RAISINS ?
1-18

"GO TO WORK!"
"AND STAY OUT OF TROUBLE!"
WELL, IT'S BETTER THAN "HAVE A NICE DAY"
1-19
DIK BROWNE
© 1988 King Features Syndicate Inc. World rights reserved

I'M AFRAID I MUST CONFIRM YOUR WORST SUSPICIONS, MADAM

YOU DO, INDEED, HAVE TERMITES
DIK BROWNE 1-20

SURE, THE RICH HAVE MONEY AND LUXURY AND POWER —BUT— DO YOU THINK THEY'RE HAPPY ?

WELL...
I DON'T WANT TO HEAR!!
DIK BROWNE
1-21

THAT LITTLE PUPPY IS GOING TO BE A BIG DOG SOMEDAY!
HOW DO YOU KNOW?

DIK BROWNE
1-22
YOU CAN ALWAYS TELL BY THE SIZE OF THEIR PAWS

NO! AND I AIN'T CHANGING MY MIND!

HOW ABOUT CHANGING YOUR SHIRT?
DIK BROWNE
1-23

HEY! THIS ISN'T BOILING OIL! IT'S JUST DISHWATER!
DON'T BLAME ME!

DID YOU SEE OUR OIL BILL THIS MONTH?!
1-25
DIK BROWNE

THIS IS TO DECIDE IF WOMEN ARE EQUAL TO MEN!
DIK BROWNE
OKAY—TWO OUT OF THREE!
1-26

WE ALL HAVE COLDS. HELGA, HONI, HAMLET AND ME
OKAY. THIS IS EYE OF NEWT. ALL OF YOU TAKE IT
© 1988 King Features Syndicate Inc. World rights reserved
BUT GIVE ***THIS*** TO HAMLET
ISN'T THIS EYE OF NEWT, TOO?
YES, BUT IT'S CHILDREN'S CHERRY-FLAVORED
1-27

WASTE NOT—
WANT NOT
WHAT IS
IT ?
© 1988 King Features Syndicate Inc. World rights reserved
LEFTOVER LIVER POT PIE
WANT
NOT
PIK BROWNE
1-28

ASK IF THIS IS THE ROAD TO GAUL!
ALLO! PARDONE MOI!
© 1988 King Features Syndicate, Inc. World rights reserved
VOLEZ APRES LA RUE DU GAUL SEE VOO PLAY?
SORRY, BUD, WE DON'T SPEAK FRENCH
DIK BROWNE
HE SAYS—
I KNOW, I KNOW!!
1-29

IS IT FUN GROWING UP?
YES, DEAR

BUT IT'S MORE FUN NOT TO...
DIK BROWNE
1-30

© 1988 King Features Syndicate, Inc. World rights reserved
BAM!
THAT'S BETTER
DIK BROWNE 2-8

WOMEN ARE A MYSTERY!
MEN ARE A CRIME STORY
DIK BROWNE 2-9

PLAY IT A BIT TO THE RIGHT... NOT TOO FAST... DON'T BABY, IT, EITHER...

AND DON'T CHOKE!
DIK BROWNE 2-10

DID YOU EVER WONDER HOW MEN WOULD LIVE IF IT WEREN'T FOR WOMEN ?
NO

WHAT MADE YOU THINK OF THAT ?
BROWNE 2-11

POW!
A NOTE WRAPPED AROUND A ROCK!
HOW CUTE!
IT'S A FUNNY VALENTINE

WHAT'S THAT HUMMING SOUND INSIDE THIS CAT ?
IT'S NATURAL...

THAT'S JUST THE SOUND OF THE CAT'S BODY MANUFACTURING CUTENESS
DIK BROWNE 2-13

THAT DOES IT! WE'RE GETTING YOU GLASSES!
DIK BROWNE 2·15
© 1988 King Features Syndicate, Inc. World rights reserved

THIS IS THE OLDEST GUARD DOG IN NORWAY

WOW! DOES HE BITE?
HE GUMS
DIK BROWNE 2-16

AH! MOTHER NATURE!

SPLAT!
DIK BROWNE

...A TOUGH MOTHER!
2-17

HOW'S THE DIET GOING?
SLAM!
DIK BROWNE
GOING, GOING, GONE
SLAM!
2-18

GOOD, BUT IT NEEDS MORE AGING
DIK BROWNE 2-19

ARE YOU GOING TO SLEEP ALL DAY OR ARE YOU GOING TO GET UP AND PAINT THE HOUSE ?!
TALK ABOUT QUESTIONS THAT DON'T NEED AN ANSWER !
DIK BROWNE 2·20
© 1988 King Features Syndicate, Inc. World rights reserved

THRU' THE TUNNEL AND MAKE A BOW...
©1988 King Features Syndicate Inc World rights reserved
TIE THE LOOP AND THERE YOU GO!
I DID IT!!
2-22
DIK BROWNE

DADDY'S GOT SPAGHETTI STAINS ON EVERY SINGLE BIT OF CLOTHING...COAT, SHIRT, PANTS, EVEN HIS **SHOELACES!** HE DIDN'T MISS A SPOT!

HE'S A PERFECTIONIST
2-23

WHY IS THIS CALLED HUNGARIAN GOULASH ?
THAT'S EASY

2-24
IF WE CALLED IT NORWEGIAN GOULASH WHO'D BUY IT ?
DIK BROWNE

YOU KNOW WHY I LIKE DOGS ? DOGS DON'T HAVE OPINIONS
© 1988 King Features Syndicate Inc World rights reserved
YAP YAP YAP YAP YAP!
WHO ASKED YOU ?!
2·25

THERE'S ONLY ROOM FOR ONE BOSS IN THIS HOUSE!
© 1988 King Features Syndicate Inc World rights reserved

I DEMAND A RECOUNT!
2-26 DIK BROWNE

BIG ICEBERG!
© 1988 King Features Syndicate Inc World rights reserved
BAM!
DIK BROWNE
2·27
TOUGH BOAT!

©1988 King Features Syndicate, Inc. World rights reserved
HEY, MR. ARTIST! CAN WE BORROW YOUR LADDER?
2-29
DIK BROWNE

IF YOU CAN'T SAY SOMETHING NICE ABOUT MY MOTHER DON'T SAY ANYTHING AT ALL!!
DIK BROWNE 3-1
THAT WAS UNCALLED FOR!

PLINK!
PLINK!
SPRING FEVER
3-2
DIK BROWNE
© 1988 King Features Syndicate Inc. World rights reserved

YOU OVERSLEPT AGAIN!
I NEVER OVERSLEEP.
GETTING UP AT NOON IS VERY NATURAL FOR ME
DIK BROWNE
3-3

THAT CREEP JUST ASKED FOR A PIÑA COLADA WITH A PAPER PARASOL, A CHERRY AND A STRAW
© 1988 King Features Syndicate Inc World rights reserved

SOUNDS GOOD! GET ME ONE, TOO!
GOOD CHOICE
DIK BROWNE 3-4

HOW ABOUT AN APPETIZER?
OKAY, BUT NO SOUP!

I GOTTA LEAVE ROOM FOR DESSERT
DIK BROWNE 3-5

MAMA
MIA!!
OH, COME ON!
WE'RE NOT THAT
HEAVY!!
3-7
DIK
BROWNE
© 1988 King Features Syndicate Inc. World rights reserved

WILL YOU TELL THIS GUY TO STOP BUGGING ME!
PLINK!
NO WAY!

YOU'RE THE ONE WHO ASKED HIM TO PASS THE NUTS
3-8
PAH-FOOF!
KLINK!
NUTS
DIK BROWNE

THIS IS GREAT!
YEAH! AND HELGA MAKES IT ALL FROM SCRATCH!

SCRATCH
3-9 DIK BROWNE

HE HAS PARROT FEVER
CAN WE DO ANYTHING FOR HIM ?

I DON'T KNOW— IT MAY BE TOO LATE
3-10 DIK BROWNE

GIMME A WHISKEY AND A SPLASH OF WATER
RIGHTO!
© 1988 King Features Syndicate Inc World rights reserved
SPLASH!
DIK BROWNE
NEW BARTENDER
3-11

YOUR TAXES ARE DUE
SORRY, IT'S BEEN A TOUGH YEAR, SO I WON'T BE ABLE TO PAY MY TAXES THIS YEAR

DID I SAY SOMETHING FUNNY ?
3-12
DIK BROWNE

IS THAT YOU, DEAR ?
?!!!
DIK BROWNE
3-14
© 1988 King Features Syndicate Inc World rights reserved

SPRING'S COMING
YEAH, I GUESS "OLD MAN WINTER" IS DEAD!
SPLAT!
DIK BROWNE
NOTHING PERSONAL
3-15

A PENNY FOR YOUR THOUGHTS

FORGET IT
DIK BROWNE 3-16

UH-OH!
GOTCHA LEPRECHAUN !! GIMME YOUR GOLD OR I WON'T SET YOU FREE! WHAT DO YOU SAY?
I DEMAND A LAWYER
DIK BROWNE 3-17

IT SAYS "PUT ALL YOUR MONEY IN HERE"
IS THAT IT?

I WISH THEY'D MAKE TAX INSTRUCTIONS SIMPLER
PUT ALL YOUR MONEY IN HERE
3-18

"SAY AH"

IT'S CONTAGIOUS ISN'T IT, DOCTOR ?
BANG! BANG!